WISDOM'S WHIT

Wisdom's Whit

Co-Editor Angela Lusardi

ISBN: 1890306940

Library of Congress Control Number: 2005937957

*I would like to thank all of the writers
I have quoted from in my collection of poems.
Again, a special thank you to my dear wife
for her guidance and wisdom.*

Warwick House Publishers
720 Court Street
Lynchburg, VA 24504

Contents

The sweetest soul
that ever look'd with human eyes.
—ALFRED, LORD TENNYSON
"IN MEMORIAM"

I dedicate this book in loving memory of my father,
Vincent Joseph Lusardi, Sr.
(1916-1983)
"Old Blue Eyes"

Beyond the bright searchlights of science,
Out of sight of the windows of sense,
Old riddles still bid us defiance,
Old questions of Why and of Whence.
—WILLIAM WHETHAM
"THE RECENT DEVELOPMENT OF PHYSICAL SCIENCE"

I

DEEPER QUESTIONS

Who am I?
Where do I belong?
So many questions blowing through
Time,
Too few souls with peace of mind.
Yet, it's the questions of the deep
That shall awaken us from
Our sleep.
The answers to life's dark mysteries
Lie quietly within.
For it is Here,
Where we are destined to become
One with Him.

A Questioning Manner

Religion beats me.
I'm amazed at folk drinking the gospels in
And never scratching their heads for questions.
—SIEGFRIED SASSOON

Are the faithful those who never doubt
Never pondering what life is about?
Faith is a wonderful thing.
Yet equally important
Is what you have placed your trust in.
Question your Holy Bible and Koran,
Challenge every woman and mortal man.
Doubt every truth
You have ever been taught,
Dissect each and every sacred part.
Out of this eternal probing
Shall spring forth the Wisdom Tree,
A golden stairway leading toward Thee.

Blessed are those who faithfully doubt:
For within their questioning
Shall find their way out.

Wrestling with God

Doubt is the sign of an unsure mind,
Yet within our despair
We are destined to climb.

I am a poet who doubts,
A modern day Thomas working his way out.
Like a mustard seed I toil through the sod,
Struggling daily with my conceptions of God.
And as I grow
I let go of broken dreams, shattered views,
And childish beliefs of Eternal You.
Yet, no matter how high I climb
Toward Heavenly Mind,
A bit of doubt is always there
Clinging tenaciously to my faithful prayer.

The Thinker

Who breathes must suffer,
And who thinks must mourn;
And he alone is bless'd
Who ne'er was born.
— MATTHEW PRIOR

There are times when I wish I had
Remained ignorant and blind,
A narrow-minded fool
Traveling through time.
It is far easier to accept
What we've been taught,
Than it is to challenge
Every sacred part.
Yet once the Questioning Box is cracked,
There is no turning back.
No longer will a soul be content
Within his dark cave,
It's only through wisdom are we saved.
No longer will a soul reach behind,
Only by moving forward
Does one awaken to The Divine.

A Comic Quest

Man with his burning soul
Has but an hour of breath
To build a ship of Truth
In which his soul may sail...
—<small>JOHN MASEFIELD</small>
"<small>TRUTH</small>"

Is it possible to find God alone?
Does one need help finding
His way Home?
How did Jesus awaken
To the Light within?
Did he have a teacher guiding him?
Do all Christians become a Christ?
Does every non-Christian
Inherit Eternal life?
Has Truth been placed in the Bible,
Torah, and Koran?
Is Wisdom's beauty available
To every woman and man?
These questions, they fill my sail,
Propelling my soul through the sea
Of hell.

Eternal Questions

What endless questions vex the thought,
Of Whence, and Whither,
When and How?
—Sir Richard Francis Burton

One plus one equals two.
Two plus two equals four.
Three plus three leads through
Yet, another door.
The answers to life's questions
Never please, they merely tease,
Continuing to vex,
Propelling humankind to solve mysteries
That become increasingly complex.
Like a Divine Wind,
The questions never end,
Only by questioning does one awaken
From within.

A Faithful Questioner

Always the beautiful answer
Who asks a more beautiful question.
—EDWARD E. CUMMINGS
"INTRODUCTION TO COLLECTED POEMS"

If every soul perceived a lie to be true,
Would what is True
Still shine through?
From where does Truth come?
Does it radiate from a Perfect One?
And who is Christ?
Is it Jesus alone,
Or a gathering of perfect souls
Calling Heaven Eternal Home?
So many questions.
Yet, it's questioning that leads to a
Higher perception.
The more questions we faithfully ask,
The closer we are
To fulfilling our mortal task.

Prisoners of Time

The sand of the sea and the raindrops,
And the days of eternity, who can assess them?
The height of the sky and the breadth of the earth,
And the depth of the abyss, who can probe them?
— ECCLESIASTICUS

"As I think so shall I be,"
Is a quote that not only puzzles
But at times torments me.
For, how much power do we truly possess,
Our ancient souls who long to bless?
How does one find Peace of Mind,
Awaken to the Divine?
When one deals with an illness related
To the brain,
When one struggles daily with bodily pain?
Are we prisoners of time,
Captors to the body and mind?
These questions, they haunt humankind,
These lonely doubts of mine.

Prisoners of Pain

I have known no man of genius who had
Not to pay, in some affliction or
Defect either physical or spiritual,
For what the gods had given him.
—Sir Max Beerbohm

I cannot describe the despair I feel,
The hopelessness of being ill.
Daily I carry a cross of pain and fatigue,
A darkness which seldom takes leave.
A thousand days I have cried,
A thousand more I shall contemplate suicide.
Will my journey ever become
Cheerful and bright,
Forever free from the sorrow of the night?
Only time shall tell
As I continue my journey through
The depths of hell.

Stranger at the Door

I came as a stranger
And I shall leave as a stranger.
—THE LAST WORDS SPOKEN BY
DR. GEORGE WYCLIFFE
(1897)

Who am I?
Am I this restless mind
Who ponders why?
Am I this fragile body
Which shall wither and die?
Am I the glorious sun which brightly burns?
Am I this dark anger which slowly churns?
Really, who am I?
Am I the sum of those things or much more?
I hope I am beyond,
For these so-called things live on borrowed time.
But the mystery still remains,
Who are we?
Is it Almighty God who envisions you and me?
Was it several gods who created humankind?
Or was it simply an accident—
This thing called time?

The Mysterious Heavens

There are more things in heaven and earth,
Horatio,
Than are dreamt of in your philosophy.
—WILLIAM SHAKESPEARE

Imagine one's soul without a body
And a face,
An Eternity blessed with Heavenly Grace.
Imagine a loved one as a beam
Of light,
A soul mate with unlimited sight.
It's nearly impossible for the human mind
To clearly perceive.
Under the yoke of dogma one has little
If any,
Freedom to breathe.
Truth is a stranger to you and me,
A foreigner is the Light of Eternity.

There is nothing so powerful as truth,
—and often nothing so strange.
—DANIEL WEBSTER

The Tree of Wisdom

There is no unbelief;
Whoever plants a seed beneath the sod
And waits to see it push away the clod,
He trusts in God.
　　　　　—Lizzie York Case
　　　　　"Unbelief"

We must believe,
Yet we must question our human creeds.
As we question, we slowly grow,
And as we transcend, we evolve,
Until at last we shall reach that point
Where all mysteries have been truly solved.
A complete understanding with the Divine
Is the pinnacle of space and time.

Truth…it is the highest summit of art
And of life.
　　　　　—Henri-Frédéric Amiel

A Journey Through the Mind

We shall not cease in our explorations,
And the end of our exploring
Will be to arrive where we started
And to know the place for the first time.
—T. S. ELIOT

Today is tomorrow's past,
The rim of the circle which doesn't last.
And as the circle of life expands,
So sails the ship of man.
Until at last the universe shall collapse
And return to where it began,
The eye of the storm
A center of Heavenly Calm.

Awakening to the Divine.
It shall be like falling in love
For the first time.

For I dipt into the future, far as human eye could see,
Saw the Vision of the world,
And all the wonder that would be...
—Alfred, Lord Tennyson

II

FAMILY WHIT:
AN EMERGING VIEW

There shall arise from this confused
Sound of voices
A firmer faith than that our fathers knew,
A deep religion which alone rejoices
In worship of the Infinitely True.
—SIR LEWIS MORRIS
"BROTHERHOOD"

Blind Obedience

He who serves our Führer, Adolf Hitler,
Serves Germany,
And he who serves Germany serves God.
—Baldur Von Schirach (1936)

Who determines who is our enemy
And who is our friend,
When it is time to attack and time to defend?
And, who is a Patriot?
Is it someone who never questions
And blindly obeys?
Like a common slave he marches
To his grave.
Patriotism is like a two-edged sword.
That which has the power to defend
Our freedom and joy,
Also carries the potential to completely destroy.

A patriot is a fool in ev'ry age.
—Alexander Pope

The Beast

We have buried the putrid corpse
of liberty.
　　　　　　—Benito Mussolini

How does one remain in a peaceful state,
When one is constantly guarding
Against those filled with hate?
The defenders of Freedom will never bring
A permanent peace.
For they, like the aggressor,
Are part of the beast.
Yet, if we turn the other cheek we will
Likely be destroyed,
Along with our freedom and children's joy.
So the question remains,
How does one live with a hungry beast,
When what he desires is you
As his Feast?

The Face of Ignorance

The devil can cite Scripture for his purpose.
—WILLIAM SHAKESPEARE

Ben Laden and the Taliban
Faithfully quote from the Holy Koran.
The Christian Crusaders who invaded the
Middle East.
How easily they killed and plundered
In the name of Peace.
The KKK
Hold their Bibles firmly in hand,
While they preach the superiority
Of the white man.
The ignorant can cite Scripture as easily
As the wise.
Yet one seeks to enslave,
While the other struggles to enlighten
And save.

A Falling Temple

Pillars are falling at thy feet,
Fanes quiver in the air,
A prostrate city is thy seat,
And thou alone art there.
—Lydia M. Child
"Marius Amid the Ruins of Carthage"

The war has begun
The battles between father and son.
Thousands have died,
Thousands more are being crucified.
Muslims are killing Jews,
Christians are slaughtering Hindus.
All in the name of god,
A tribal god who seeks to destroy
Happiness and eternal joy.
And as the religious wars rage on
So crumbles the temple of man,
For a house divided cannot stand.

If a house be divided against itself,
that house cannot stand.
—Jesus

The Peacemakers

We must conquer war,
Or war will conquer us.
—ELY CULBERTSON
"MUST WE FIGHT RUSSIA?"

How easily we forget
That monsters who are cruel and mean
Are also human beings.
No matter how vicious a person may become,
To someone she or he was a daughter or son.
So, each sunrise we must decide
Whether to follow the Prince of Peace
Or our never-ending pride.
We can deliver to the world healing love,
Or continue to drop bombs from above.

Blessed are the peacemakers:
For they shall be called the children of God.
—JESUS

Everlasting Mercy

Justice is the only worship.
Love is the only priest.
Ignorance is the only slavery.
Happiness is the only good.
        —ROBERT GREEN INGERSOLL
            "CREED"

I pray that the Kingdom of God
Is a perfect state where Liberty sings.
I hope that the crown of eternal joy
Is not worn by one or two kings.
I pray that the heart of God is pure love
An everlasting mercy descending from above.
I hope that ignorance will come to its end,
And true happiness spreads
From friend to friend.
I pray that love becomes the only priest,
I pray and hope for the end of the beast.

A Peopled Garden

The one great God looked down and smiled,
And counted each His loving child;
For Turk and Brahmin, monk and Jew,
Had reached Him through the gods they knew.
—HARRY ROMAINE

As long as religions crusade to convert
There will never be peace on earth.
One doesn't find God by changing another,
One embraces the Divine
By celebrating the diversity of humankind.
If God had not wanted Buddha to
Teach humankind,
Buddha would have been destroyed
When his body was the size of a dime.
If God had not wanted Islam to be born,
He would have plucked
This rose and thorn.
God bless diversity!
A colorful garden of Christian, Muslim, and Jew,
A beautiful rainbow celebrating You.

A Family of One

All your strength is in your union.
All your danger is in discord;
Therefore be at peace henceforward,
And as brothers live together.
          —LONGFELLOW
      "THE SONG OF HIAWATHA"

Islam is not out to destroy Christianity
And the Bible does not disprove the Koran.
Every faith has been blessed
With Grace,
Serving a different branch of the human race.
The religions of the world enhance
One another,
Like a loving family of sister and brother…
What one lacks, the other gives,
And together, in harmony, we freely live.

Heaven on Earth

I got a religion that wants to take heaven
Out of the clouds
And plant it right here on the earth
Where most of us can get a slice of it.
—IRWIN SHAW

If you were the guardian of Heaven's Gate
What kind of Paradise would you create?
Would you welcome all
From the frailest of the small
To the tallest of the tall?
Would you accept every branch of the religious tree
From Judaism to Christianity?
Would you freely embrace every color
Of the human race
From ebony to the whitest of lace?
Would you offer sanctuary to the common
Woman and man,
A safe haven to all who stand?
Or would you love only the Christian best
And to hell you would send the rest?

Hell on Earth

The heart of man is the place
The Devil dwells in:
I feel sometimes a hell within myself.
—Sir Thomas Browne
(1605-1682)

Hell is where we make the same mistake
Over and over again.
Continuing the same cycle
Of sorrow and pain.
Yet, how does one break free?
How does one break the ball and chain
Of uncertainty?
We seek Wisdom from above
And Guidance from within,
We need help from brother and friend.
A man can never rise above alone,
A woman needs a helping hand
To find her way home.
Together, like a field of flowers,
We are destined to thrive,
Together, as a diverse race,
We shall come alive.

An Understanding Heart

Teach me to feel another's woe,
To hide the fault I see;
That mercy I to others show,
That mercy show to me.
—ALEXANDER POPE
"THE UNIVERSAL PRAYER"

For those who have never doubted
The existence of a compassionate God,
Take heed my friend.
It's not a matter of if,
It's just a matter of when.
And when you fall
You shall at last understand,
Within your grief, your heart shall expand.
You shall feel the hopelessness of night,
Embracing why a person would
Take his life.
You shall come to know the beast,
The great destroyer of tranquility and peace.
And within compassion shown
Your heart shall find its home.

Coming of Age

Everything is in a state of metamorphosis.
Thou thyself art in everlasting change...

—MARCUS AURELIUS
"MEDITATIONS"

As a young child
I was taught to believe in a Father
Who judges and condemns,
A tribal god
Who accepts only Christian women and men.
Yet, as I grew,
So evolved my perceptions of You.
Now I believe in a Loving Being
Who accepts all,
From the lowest of the low
To the tallest of the tall.
In my heart
There dances Christian, Muslim, and Jew.
Within my eyes
There shines but one family magnifying You.

...Together let us extol his name.

—PSALMS

Deep into that darkness peering,
Long I stood there,
Wondering, fearing,
Doubting, dreaming dreams no mortal
Ever dared to dream before.
—EDGAR ALLAN POE
"THE RAVEN"

III

GOSPEL'S VISION

Listen!
I am a poet who has something to say,
Whose poetry challenges the current
Thinking of today.
I believe Truth has been placed in the
Bible, Torah, and Koran.
I believe Wisdom is available to every
Woman and man.
I believe every Christian shall become
A Christ,
All non-Christians shall inherit
Eternal Life.
I am a poet with a Heavenly Vision,
Whose poems challenge every
Narrow-minded religion.

The Martyrs

To know how to say what other people only think,
Is what makes men poets and sages;
And to dare to say what others only dare to think,
Makes men martyrs or reformers.
—Elizabeth R. Charles

Human beings will make you a glorious god
If you give them what they desire.
Yet, tell them what they do not want to hear
And they will set you afire.
How many souls have perished at the stake
Due to humankind's ignorance and hate?
Thousands have been crucified,
Millions have died,
And many more are yet to be cast aside.
The world at large, seeks not change,
It longs to remain the ignorant same.
And when a messenger reflects Light
Into their comfortable cave,
They seek revenge on He who came to save.

A Rude Awakening

There are certain persons for whom
Pure Truth is a poison.
—André Maurois

The world believes what it has been
Taught to believe
And, if what the world believes isn't true,
Then the human race doesn't want
To know the real You.
Humankind has grown comfortable
In its dark cave,
Blindly believing it is saved.
Our greatest fear isn't the darkness of the night,
We are terrified of awaking
To the Eternal Light.
Yet, one by one, we are forced out of our cave,
Into the Light where all are saved.

Nothing is stronger than custom.
—Ovid

He Who Strives with God

Every tiny step forward in the world
Was formerly made at the cost
Of mental and physical torture.
—FRIEDRICH WILHELM NIETZSCHE

It's hard to let go,
It is painful to grow.
It takes courage to shed familiar fears,
Family views held for hundreds,
If not thousands of years.
Think of the turmoil Buddha went through
As he blazed a path toward You.
Imagine the darkness Jesus had to overcome
As he labored his way under the hot Judean sun.
Conceive of Mohammad's pain
As he created a new religion in God's name.
Growing pains, part of our heritage,
Our common name.

Love overcomes all obstacles.
—VIRGIL

The Blessed Discontented

The world owes all its onward impulses
To men ill at ease.
The happy man inevitably confines
Himself within ancient limits.
—NATHANIEL HAWTHORNE

The comfortable, contented will never
Let go.
It's the dissatisfied who are destined
To grow.
It's the disillusioned who challenge
Political and religious lines,
Who expand
The awareness of humankind.
If every man and woman were content
The world would never grow.
The Glory of God
We would never come to know.

Rebels with a Cause

No hell!
Rang out the Universalist bell.
—GEORGE W. BUNGAY
"THE CREEDS OF THE BELLS"

We are rebels who faithfully yell,
"We do not believe in an eternal hell!"
"We believe all are destined
To drink from the Holy Grail!"
Yet, the preacher says the Bible
Is filled with hell fire,
And universal salvation is merely
Our own desire.
We are gadflies who courageously rebel
Against all who believe in an
Eternal hell!

The most frightful idea that has ever
corroded human nature—
The idea of eternal punishment.
—JOHN, VISCOUNT MORLEY

Unmasking the Devil

Speak the truth and shame the Devil.
—FRANCOIS RABELAIS
(1495-1553)

It is our mortal task,
We are here to remove the shadowy mask:
The mask of fear,
The mask of chaos lurking ever near.
The devil is a metaphor symbolizing
All that is cruel and mean,
A mask worn by every human being.
Beyond the illusion of time
Shines the Divine,
Forever smiling beyond the madness
Of humankind.

An Eternal Vigil

With Ignorance wage eternal war,
To know thyself for ever strain,
Thine ignorance of thine ignorance
Is thy fiercest foe, thy deadliest bane.
—Sir Richard F. Burton

To offend the least,
I have been told,
Should be the journey of every soul.
Yet, what if the world sees hate as love
And night as day,
How then will we ever find our way?
Sometimes we must cruelly offend,
In order to awaken others from within.

The Sword of Christ

*I once had a dream,
And in my vision I saw a sword of ice
Being wielded by a Crystal Christ.
With Eternity behind him
He plunged his dagger into the heart
Of Falsehood,
And out of our shattered world came
Forth a true brotherhood.
A perfect universe of endless blue,
A peaceful race, forever, celebrating You.*

Metamorphosis

I held it truth, with him who sings
To one clear harp in divers tones,
That men may rise on stepping stones
Of their dead selves to higher things.
—ALFRED, LORD TENNYSON

Each day part of us dies!
And upon this dead self we arise.
We build upon the broken and old,
Upon the shattered we climb toward Heavenly Soul.
Like the four seasons we let go
Our hopes and dreams,
Dark lies and never-ending schemes.
Until at last,
Humankind shall shed its final sin,
And joyfully awaken to the Christ within!

Imagine

To know is nothing at all;
To imagine is everything.
—ANATOLE FRANCE

Like a spoiled child there are times
When I think I know it all.
Then I listen to an Enlightened One
And realize how little I truly understand,
How much more my imagination needs
To expand.
To know is nothing at all,
Compared to the Divine
The human mind is small.
To imagine is to break free,
And continue our journey to Eternal Thee.
For what is Paradise?
It's the imagination of the Divine,
Eternal Truth shining beyond the
Darkness of time.

The Starving Artist

Rather than love, than money, than fame,
Give me truth.
—HENRY DAVID THOREAU

I hunger not for glory and fame,
I am starved for my Eternal Name.
I desire not silver or gold,
I am lonely for my Heavenly Soul.
I long not to live in a human cage,
I yearn to be free of rage.
I thirst not for bottled wine,
I am thirsty for the Divine.

The Waters of Wisdom

Blessed are they which do hunger
And thirst after righteousness:
For they shall be filled.
—JESUS
"GOSPEL OF MATTHEW"

Dip into the wisdom pool,
Its waters are refreshingly cool.
The waters of Enlightenment shall quench
Your wizened thirst,
Bringing healing to that which has been cursed.
Wisdom's well excludes not the religiously small,
But freely embraces Eternal All.
The waters of wisdom fall as Heavenly Dew,
Delivering salvation to all who
Thirst for You.

My cup runneth over.
—PSALMS

A Single Soul Satisfying Thought

One single soul satisfying thought
Can shatter the heart.

Living within the confines of tradition
Maintains the status quo.
It's thinking outside the current circle
Where the human race is able to grow.
One spontaneous thought can transform
Our awareness of Soul,
Spreading like wildfire from the young
To the very old.
Fresh ideas open our hearts to new ways
Of Being,
Liberating our closed minds to a higher way
Of Seeing.

Through the Eyes of Wisdom

To see clearly is poetry, prophecy, and religion,
All in one.
                                        —JOHN RUSKIN

Many grow old,
And some become vaguely wise.
Even fewer learn to see
With clarity in their eyes.
Truly perceiving is the potential
Of humankind,
Clearly seeing is to awaken
To the Divine.
Within our Father's mind
There exists no division between
Daughter and Son,
Within His Eyes
All shine as Holy One.

Blessed are the pure in heart:
For they shall see God.
                                        —JESUS

The Search for Truth is like
Giving birth.
Out of great suffering comes forth
A babe,
The Light of Wisdom destined
To save.

IV

Journey to the Stars:
I Am the Way

She is a reflection of the eternal light...
—Wisdom

There is a Calm within
Which shines from beyond.
A quiet stillness breaking
Through our darkest sorrow.
A beacon of Light beckoning humankind
Toward what is
And what shall be...
A hopeful tomorrow
Laced with Heavenly Thee.

The Lighthouse

Ye are the light of the world.
—JESUS

The Light of Christ accepts members
From every faith,
Every soul who carries the human weight.
It doesn't matter where you have been
Nor what you have done,
The Isle of Christ embraces all as Holy One.
Daily shine His brilliant beams,
Upon these lightways travel our hopes and dreams.
Each Light is a ray of Heavenly Gold
Destined to bring home the wandering soul.

The Crystal Christ

Far, far the mountain peak from me
Where lone He stands, with look caressing;
I lift my dreaming eyes and see
His hand stretched forth in blessing.
—FLORENCE E. COATES
"THE CHRIST OF THE ANDES"

High above
Shines the Crystal Christ,
A perfect being of Sweetness and Light.
Daily we meditate upon his Heavenly Soul,
Ever so slowly
Our awareness is uplifted beyond the human hold.
We are destined to become
What we gaze upon,
A Christ, a Star,
A Heavenly Son.

Heavenly Ambition

To be what we are,
And to become what we are capable of becoming,
Is the only end of life.
—Robert Louis Stevenson
"Familiar Studies of Men and Books"

As an embryo what do you
Aspire to be?
As for me, I desire to be free.
But, how does one find such peace,
By roaming, by sitting still,
By listening to our Father's will?
Some find Salvation by falling from
The sky,
Others achieve Nirvana by climbing
Heavenly high.
The paths to God are infinite
Like the stars in the skies.
Yet all roads lead to Heaven,
Our eternal prize.

Rejoice because your names are written
in the stars!

Children of the Light

Like the flower our soul strives to become one
With the Eternal Light,
Like a tiny mustard seed it struggles
To break free of the night.
Ever so gently unfolds the human soul
For our destiny is Heavenly Gold.
When the last of the dreamers has awakened from the night,
When the last soul has taken flight,
Judgment Day will have its say:
All are children of the Light,
Each is precious in his Sight.
None kneel below,
Not one stands above,
All are destined for Eternal Love.

Gatherers of the Light

Nothing is so like a soul as a bee.
It goes from flower to flower as a soul
From star to star,
And it gathers honey as a soul gathers light.
— Victor Hugo

From flower to flower buzzes the bee,
From star to star journey you and me.
The bees gather nectar making sweet honey
While the human race gathers light
Bringing hope into the darkest night.
Together, as winged souls, we can create
A perfect garden,
A paradise blessed with Heavenly Pardon.

...together let us extol his name.
— Psalms

The Man in the Moon

But sometimes, through the Soul of Man,
Slow moving o'er his pain,
The moonlight of a perfect peace
Floods heart and brain.
—WILLIAM SHARP
"THE WHITE PEACE"

Even into the darkest night
The sun sends its healing light.
By the way of the moon
It reflects into our life.
Soft, yet strong, it smiles,
A mysterious soul shining like highest noon.
And as the man in the moon
Comes to his end,
Our awareness of his brother, the sun,
Arises from within.

Facing Our Fears

The thing that numbs the heart is this:
That men cannot devise
Some scheme of life to banish fear
That lurks in most men's eyes.
—James Norman Hall
"Fear"

We flee from sorrow and pain,
Desperately trying to escape from that
Which is part of our name.
One cannot hide from the storms within,
One must bravely transcend.
We must bring to the surface
The demons of the night,
And our fears shall disappear into
The Eternal Light.

There is no fear in love;
But perfect love casteth out fear.
—John

The Lantern

He held the lamp of Truth that day
So low that none could miss the way;
And yet so high to bring in sight
That picture fair—the World's Great Light—
—W. G. ELMSLIE
"THE HAND THAT HELD IT"

What is Faith?
The journey of Faith is a pilgrim traveling
Through a dream,
Following a lantern held by a hand unseen.
Wherever the Light moves he or she shall follow,
Faithfully journeying toward
A HeavenlyTomorrow.

Faith is the substance of things hoped for,
The evidence of things not seen.
—HEBREWS

My Beloved

You are wholly beautiful, my love,
And without a blemish.
—THE SONG OF SONGS

My Beloved is not pleasure or things,
She's the joy Salvation brings.
My True Love is a fulfilled state of mind,
Forever shining as the Christ Divine.
My Soul mate possesses
Neither a body nor face,
She smiles as Eternal Grace.
It shall be love at first sight
Awakening to Her Light!

The Eternal Feminine draws us on.
—GOETHE

The Light of Grace

As long as there is a soul to reach,
The Light of Wisdom shall joyfully teach.

The Light of Wisdom, Heaven's Grace,
Is destined to free the human race.
The meticulous chains,
Along with what we perceive
As eternal gain,
Shall be shattered into a trillion stars.
There will be no hideous scars
Within our ancient
Yet new-born freedom,
There will shine but Wisdom, Herself,
Quietly lighting our path.

Crystal Clear

For each age is a dream that is dying,
Or one that is coming to birth.
—Arthur O'Shaughnessy

An epiphany in space,
I once dreamt of Heavenly Grace.
What I saw
Was a stream of tiny white lights.
Traveling to and from the earth,
A never-ending cycle of death and birth.
From whither these souls came
I do not know.
Yet where they go
All are destined to show.
The Eye of Calm,
The Heart of Christ,
Forever shining into the endless night.

The Book of Life

For every star sparkling in the skies,
There shines a precious soul within our
Father's Eyes.

Infinite is the Book of Life,
Forever shining
As the Light of Christ.
Whenever a soul
Is added to the ancient scroll
The List of Life quietly unrolls.
And, as each dreamer awakens to the Divine,
The Lights of Heaven twinkle in time.

Rejoice because your names are written
in the Book of Life!

A Beautiful Dream

I once dreamt of a Crystal Christ
A perfect being of Sweetness and Light.

During the day I give my body and mind
To the labors of time.
Yet during the night I offer myself
To the teachings of the Divine.
Quietly it reaches into my dreams
Shedding light upon my inner screams.
One such powerful dream came years ago
During a January night of falling snow.

There I sat in the lotus seat
With Jesus kneeling at my feet.
Yet the figure I saw was not composed
Of flesh and bone
But of diamond-like gems,
Symbolizing the Eternal Christ within.
Gently, Jesus bent over and kissed my feet,
And within that Holy Moment
I shined complete.

A Singular Purpose

He saw an overwhelming need,
It filled his heart with searching fire;
He gave himself, his time, his wealth,
To realize his heart's desire.
—JOHN OXENHAM

Into this world he was born,
A little babe destined to wear a
Crown of thorns.
Though his years numbered a mere thirty-three,
His brief dance blazed a glorious trail
Toward Heavenly Thee.

He is our teacher, poet, and brother,
A beloved soul like no other.
Within the sands of time he stands
Brilliantly tall,
Yet beyond he is as equal as Heavenly All.
Jesus is who all are destined to become
A Christ, A Savior
A Perfect Son.

…no longer a Christian, but a Christ.
—GOSPEL OF PHILIP

Strength is made perfect in weakness.
—Corinthians

V

CARRIERS OF THE LIGHT

The race is not to the swift,
Nor the battle to the strong.
—ECCLESIASTES

Emily Dickinson never climbed
The ladder of success,
Yet one hundred years later her poetry
Shines as some of the best.
From his writings, Thoreau never made a dime,
Yet today millions read him
As a beautiful mind.
Earless Van Gogh went madly insane,
And now the world celebrates his
Brilliant name.

The Enlightened Ones

(Their) love was like the liberal air, —
Embracing all, to cheer and bless;
And every grief that mortals share
Found pity in (their) tenderness.
　　　　　　—WILLIAM WINTER

Buddha delivered wisdom to the human heart,
And six-hundred years later
Jesus played his healing part.
Both men burned with a fire
To free humankind from its dark desire.
And so the time honored tradition
Of healing goes on,
Singing a never-ending song.
Each person is born with a talent
Of inward gold,
And it is up to each to develop
His Vision of soul.
We can either use our powers to destroy,
Or like Buddha and Jesus,
We can deliver happiness and eternal joy.

A Painful Choice

The difficulty in life is the choice.
—GEORGE MOORE

The ego seeks to control,
While our soul longs to relinquish its human hold.
The ego loves to dominate others,
While our soul desires equality between
Sisters and brothers.
Two voices yet, but one choice.
We can either follow the ego,
Or glorify God by letting go.
For the smaller our egos become
The closer we feel to the Eternal Son.

A Noble Path

Teach me to feel another's woe,
To hide the fault I see;
That mercy I to others show,
That mercy show to me.

—Alexander Pope
"The Universal Prayer"

The goal of the Heart is to let go,
And within our fall
We are destined to grow.
A Soul of Truth seeks not to possess,
And within our freedom we joyfully bless.
A man of Giving does not brag
About what he has done,
Within his sharing, salvation is won.
A woman of Wisdom desires not mortal fame,
And within her journey
Eternity is gained.

A Thoughtful Soul:
The Hand of God

What wisdom can you find that is
Greater than kindness?
—JEAN JACQUES ROUSSEAU

What good is a wholesome body without
A peaceful mind?
What good is Wisdom without being kind?
As one grows closer to the light,
So expands his or her compassion
For the children of the night.
A thoughtful brother feels
Another's pain and sorrow,
Embracing their hopes for a brighter tomorrow.
The Hand of God is soft, yet strong,
Powerful but tender,
To kindness the ego shall willingly surrender.

Unsung Heroes

The core of life is not silver or gold.
The essence of life is the commonplace soul.

Day by day
It's the ordinary man who delivers
Bread to a hungry world,
Moment by Moment the unknown woman
Transforms our sorrows into a radiant pearl.
Each soul is like a raindrop
Destined to fall,
For how else can the thirsty earth be saved
Except by one drop at a time,
One precious Savior held in Heavenly Mind.
I am grateful that Jesus gave his life,
And I am equally thankful
For my mother and beloved wife.

Top of the Morning

It was only a glad "Good morning,"
As she passed along the way,
But it spread the morning's glory
Over the livelong day.
—CHARLOTTE AUGUSTA
"GOOD MORNING"

A lovely smile is an expression of Grace,
A friendly hello uplifts the human race.
A smile is worth its weight in gold,
A warm heart radiates from
A soft and gentle soul.
Carrying a bright face is the highest of arts,
For it's happiness which delivers salvation
To the human heart.

One isn't properly attired,
Until one is dressed with a smile!
—ROSE REID

A Chosen Saint

The healing of the world
Is in its nameless saints.
—BAYARD TAYLOR

There was once a man who was small,
Yet within his giving he gave all.
He performed many selfless deeds,
Reaching out to hundreds of souls like you and me.
Within his brief passing
He made this world a better place,
For Heaven had blessed this soul with Healing Grace.
"We are here to enhance,"
He would say,
"So come, let us celebrate this day!"
And, when his remains were laid in the grave,
His many friends rejoiced in praise.

The world knows nothing of its greatest men.
—SIR HENRY TAYLOR

A Most Meaningful Life

I want men to remember,
When gray Death sets me free,
I was a man who had many friends,
And many friends had me.
   —John Bennett
   "I Want an Epitaph"

I can still recall the afternoon
Of my uncle's funeral.
While listening to taps I began reflecting:
What is the purpose of life
Is it climbing the ladder of success
Ever unfolding as mortal best?
Or is the greatness of a person
Measured by the joy
He or she brings into the world?
There I stood with tearful eyes,
Saying goodbye to my dear uncle
Who had touched so many lives.

The greatest joy I have in life
Is helping other people.
   —Uncle Charlie Moses

Glorifying God

Heaven does not choose its elect
From among the great and wealthy.
—WILLIAM MAKEPEACE THACKERAY
"THE VIRGINIANS"

Many seek to glorify God
By dominating others,
By winning races over their sisters
And brothers.
Many strive to sit upon a golden throne,
Being worshipped by millions of unknown.
Yet, God seeks not those who climb
The ladder of success,
He desires the common rest.

The Ladder of Success

I had Ambition,
By which sin the angels fell;
I climbed and, step by step, O Lord,
Ascended into Hell.
—WILLIAM H. DAVIES
"AMBITION"

We have a choice.
We can either climb the gilded ladder of success
Or climb the ladder of consciousness.
One is made by the human ego,
While the other is laid by the Universal Soul.
The former descends into the darkness of the night,
While the latter ascends into the Eternal Light.
The ladder of success leads to mortal fame,
While the ladder of consciousness leads
To our Eternal Name.

A Black Hole

We are the hollow men who stuff ourselves,
Hollow women who line the shelves.
We fill our lives with ambition and dreams,
Sparkling trinkets and endless schemes.
Yet, even after climbing the ladder of success
And shining as mortal best,
The emptiness remains,
Still, we cry in pain.
There is only one thing that will fill this hole,
Christ, Our Eternal Soul.

A Declaration of Freedom

Resolve to be thyself: and know, that he
Who finds himself, loses his misery.
—MATTHEW ARNOLD
"SELF-DEPENDENCE"

Heaven will grant you the Freedom
To be your true self,
To live the life
You have always dreamt about.
And who is this self?
Our Soul has no beginning or end,
Our Soul shares eternity with Him.
Your Self possesses no wall,
Your Self belongs to all.
Our Souls smile as the Eternal Son,
Forever shining as Holy One.

Let thy words be few.
　　　—ECCLESIASTES

VI

Similes of God: The Soul of Wit

Brevity is the soul of wit.
—William Shakespeare

In sixteen lines or less
I seek to express
Parables unveiling the Dark Divine,
Metaphors explaining the mysteries of time.
A good poet knows
When it is time to lay his pen down.
For the shorter his poem,
The more profound.

An Eternal Craving

Blessed are they which do hunger
And thirst after righteousness:
For they shall be filled.
—JESUS

It was the fruit of the knowledge tree
That brought down the human race.
Yet, it shall be the fruit of the Wisdom Tree
That returns us to our rightful place.
Like soul-flowers we are hungry
For the Eternal Light,
Like the tree's roots we thirst for what is right.
A wholesome faith is what we crave,
A child-like wisdom destined to save.

A Gift of Knowing

Faith is the substance of things hoped for,
The evidence of things not seen.
—HEBREWS

Like a mustard seed
Each soul is born with a gift of knowing,
A deep understanding of where it is going.
Despite long bouts of darkest doubt,
It's destined to find its way out.
What begins in the subconscious mind
Eventually grows into space and time.
And as the Trees of Wisdom slowly climb,
So blossoms peace of mind.

Simple Salvation

Heaven is not reached at a single bound...
And we mount to its summit round by round.
—Josiah G. Holland

There is no magical pill,
No simple cure for what is ill.
Simple salvation does not exist,
Like a fairy tale,
It's merely a dream built upon mist.
Eternity is not achieved in a single bound.
Happiness is found
By living one day at a time,
One precious moment held in Heavenly Mind.

The Unraveling of Soul:
A Stairway to Heaven

Bit by bit we come undone,
Day by day
As we journey toward the Son.

The journey of life is like a ball of twine.
It shall slowly unravel
Until it's a dangling thread,
A golden ladder
Ascending out of the troubles of time
And there upon each rung
One's soul shall climb,
Searching, striving, for peace of mind.

Blessings on your courage boy,
That's the way to the stars!
　　　　　　　　　　—Virgil

Seeds of Lights

Sweet are the uses of adversity;
Which, like the toad, ugly and venomous,
Wears yet a precious jewel in his head...
—WILLIAM SHAKESPEARE

A Pearl is not made overnight,
It takes years for an oyster to turn
Its sorrows into a radiant light.
So it is with the human mind...
It's we who determine the use of time.
We can transform our nightmare
Into a lovely pearl...
Out of our sadness
We shall create a most beautiful world.

Practice Makes Perfect

Out of our sadness have we made
This world so beautiful.
—STEPHEN PHILLIPS

Stroke forgiveness until it purrs
Like love.
Rub your worries until they sing
As a dove.
Stroke your sorrows until they shine
Like a pearl.
Buff your sadness until it sparkles
As a beautiful world.
Stroke eternal hope until it shimmers
Like a precious stone,
Polish your patience until it shines
As a peaceful home.

Poem inspired by the wisdom
of Donald Robert Perry Marquis.

A Golden Truth

Truth is never pure,
Seldom is it simple.
　　　　　—Oscar Wilde

The search for Truth is like digging
Through a mine.
What we seek is spiritual gold,
Freedom, our Perfect Soul.
Yet, never pure is what we find,
And seldom simple are the operations
Of the mind.
The Gold is mixed with the rock and mud
Layer upon layer of worthless crud.
It's our duty to refine,
Only through purification
Shall one awaken to the Divine.

Blessed are the pure in heart:
For they shall see God.
　　　　　—Jesus

The Eternal Sunrise

I arise, facing east,
I am asking toward the light:
I am asking that my day
Shall be beautiful with light.
　　　　—MARY H. AUSTIN
　　　　"MORNING PRAYER"

The sun is like the Divine
And the clouds, the human mind.
Through this mist the Light journeys to you,
Yet what shines
Is neither pure nor perfectly true.
The clouds of ignorance not only shut God out,
But imprison souls within,
Covering the world with the darkness of sin.
Yet, ever so slowly the clouds are destined
To dissipate,
Layer upon layer of anger and hate.
Until at last,
All the world shall see is the Perfect Son,
Shining, forever, as Holy One.

Mysteries of the Christ

Little flower—but if I could understand
What you are, root and all, and all in all,
I should know what God and man is.
—ALFRED, LORD TENNYSON

Flowers—
One of Mother Nature's loveliest hours.
You bring to the world
Colorful joy and happiness,
Delivering hope into our madness.
If only I could flower
For one glorious hour,
Then maybe I would understand
God's Mysterious Power.

Beyond Words

Beauty as we feel it is something indescribable:
What it is or what it means
Can never be said.
—GEORGE SANTAYANA

Forgiveness is like a lovely flower,
Indescribable is its healing power.
Divine love is like a singing bird,
Its beauty is beyond all mortal word.
The Heavens are like a beautiful necklace,
And each soul a perfect pearl,
Reflecting salvation into a lonely world.

A Cathedral of Light

I live and love in God's peculiar light.
—MICHELANGELO
"SONNET"

Look at a stained glass window
And tell me what you perceive.
You shall see not a single pane,
But a creation composed of many a name.
Each piece has a unique shape and color,
Like a loving family of sister and brother.
And through this window the Light
Shines collectively as One,
Forever,
Through each pane as a Perfect Son.

...together let us extol his name.
—PSALMS

86

The Sea of Togetherness

Let there be spaces in your togetherness.
—KAHLIL GIBRAN
"THE PROPHET"

Every soul has been blessed with Grace
And within our togetherness each
Has its healing space.
Every life is an island connected by
The Bridge of Christ,
Forever sharing the joys and sadness
Of Eternal Life.

Though the mills of God grind slowly,
Yet they grind exceedingly small;
Though with patience He stands waiting,
With exactness grinds He all.
—FRIEDRICH VON LOGAU
(TRANSLATION BY
HENRY WADSWORTH LONGFELLOW)

Heavenly Whit

Whit: The smallest part or particle imaginable.
—WEBSTER'S

The Voice of Wisdom is like the chirp
Of a new-born bird.
Unless one sits quietly still,
It will never be heard.

The Light of Heaven is so bright
It's invisible to the human eye.
Yet, it's the Power of God
Which lights the sky.

The seeds of Eternity are too small
To be seen,
Yet, it's the little things
That make the earth happy and green.

Our Soul carries no weight,
It's our Eternal Spirit
That passes through the eye of the needle,
Heaven's Gate.